THIS DEVOTIONAL BELONGS TO:

_____

For Mama, who taught
me to treasure the wonder of
ordinary things

EVERYDAY JOYS

Devotional

TAMA FORTNER

40 Days of Reflecting on the
Intersection of Ordinary and Divine

Ink &
Willow

CONTENTS

DEAR
FRIEND

I'M SO GRATEFUL YOU'VE CHOSEN TO JOIN ME HERE on this journey of seeking and discovering the wonder and beauty hidden in *all* the moments of life. The truth is, this little collection of what I hope are joy-filled essays actually has its roots in a less-than-joyful time. It was a time when all the many pieces of my life were crumbling and caving in on me. Or so it seemed.

Changes in the seasons of life—my own and others—had thrown me off balance and out of my routines. A once-full nest began to empty as my children grew up and into their own lives, giving me a little too much quiet time. Some relationships and responsibilities changed—and not in the way I'd hoped or planned. A pandemic came and took away gatherings and celebrations, leaving more than a little loneliness in their place. The world became overwhelming. I lost my grandmother (the last of my grandparents). I lost my dog. And I lost my sense of self and purpose. It was . . . *crushing*. Largely because it was all beyond my control.

But—and isn't that such a lovely word?—as I was walking one morning, deep in desperation, I found myself praying, "Lord, show me the joy. I need to see Your joy. I need it to be a light for my path through these overwhelming days."

And God answered my prayer.

Instantly.

That doesn't usually happen. Yet, on this day, His answer appeared right before my eyes. Literally. God pointed me to the birds who never escape His notice, the trees that clap out His praise as the wind whips through their leaves, and the wildflowers He so carefully and splendidly clothes. Did the crosses I was asked to bear disappear? No. But their heaviness was lightened by those all-around-me evidences of Him.

That morning, I began to see intersections of ordinary and divine, and now I can't stop seeing them. These glimpses of God remind me that He is at work and that I am not alone. And the knowledge of His presence—personal and purposeful—has filled me with peace and joy ever since.

Of course, this *seeing* requires intentionality. I don't know about you, but I can get caught up in the blur of life—the distractions of busyness, the weight of worries, the loss and loneliness, even the lull of leisure. I then so easily miss the gifts just waiting to be discovered in all the ordinary and not-so-ordinary moments of life. As one day fades into another, I sometimes still catch myself wondering, *Have I really lived this day? Or have I missed what matters most?*

On that morning's walk, in that desperate call to God, He opened my eyes to a new way of seeing, and I don't ever want to *not see* again. He so carefully and thoughtfully fills each moment of my life—even the dark ones and the most seemingly insignificant ones—with reasons to be joyful and discoveries to delight in, if I will simply stop to see and savor them.

Will you walk with me through these forty days of seeking and finding Him in the ordinary moments of life? You won't ever find me claiming to have it completely figured out, but I'm learning. Day by day and moment by moment. I'm learning to seek, to see, and to settle into His presence. And what I'm finding there is so wonderful I can't keep it to myself.

So, I invite you to . . .

- Pause and read one devotion each day, each week, or whenever you need a moment of rest and reconnection.
- Ponder the words and meditate on the reflection. How might it apply to your own moments?
- Pray the simple prayers.
- Consider the journaling prompts and record your thoughts and insights.
- Embrace the challenge and seek Him in the moment.

As you journey through these forty devotions, I hope and pray you'll find—as I have—that . . .

Life is best lived at the intersection of ordinary and divine.

Much love,

Tama

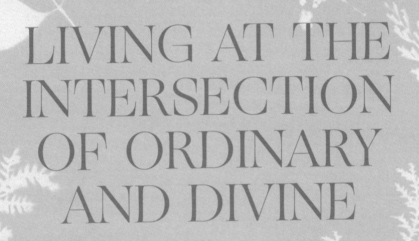

LIVING AT THE INTERSECTION OF ORDINARY AND DIVINE

Day 1

The Lord your God will be with you wherever you go.

THESE DAYS, I am trying to remember to invite God into *all* the moments of my life. Not just the big, the extraordinary, or the most desperate, but the everyday, the ordinary, and even the mundane moments as well. I want to seek His presence over Monday's breakfast and on Thursday afternoons. I've made it my goal to turn to His Word first thing each morning and to ask Him to bless my rest each night. I talk to Him in the car, in the shower, and as I write. And to my utter delight, I'm finding that He is always there. Just as He has promised to be.

Seeking God in all the many moments of my day is a practice I've been, well, *practicing* for a while now. But I didn't always. It took a few years and a few trips through the Bible to convince myself that my continual chatter and turning to Him was not just tolerated but sought, welcomed, and even treasured. (*By the Lord of All Creation! I mean, how amazing is that?*)

Of course, I'm still learning and practicing this total dependence on God. I suspect that I will be all the days of my life. But the one thing I'm seeing over and over again—the thing I am just so in awe of—is the way He always seeks to meet with me. Even when I neglect and forget Him, He pours His divine presence into my oh-so-ordinary life.

The words of Psalm 23 offer a glimpse of just how pervasive His presence is. As Christians, I sometimes think we turn to this psalm so often that it's become overly familiar, and we miss the depth of its power and promise. Just look at some of the verbs that describe what God does for us, like *leads, refreshes,* and *guides.* And the places He is with us: beside quiet waters, in the darkest valleys, and in the presence of enemies.

As God's children, we are never beyond His reach or out of His presence. And when we seek Him, there is nowhere He will not be found. We are always at the intersection of ordinary and divine.

Lord, thank You for the
divine You pour into
every moment and place
of my life. Amen.

Reflect

God does not merely tolerate our presence. He seeks,
welcomes, and treasures time spent with us!

Read Psalm 139:1–12. What do these verses say to you about the presence of God in your life?

_____

_____

_____

_____

_____

_____

Compare the words of Joshua 1:9 with the words of Matthew 28:20. Who spoke each of those promises? When were they spoken? What does that tell you about the faithfulness of God and His promises?

_____

_____

_____

_____

_____

_____

_____

Challenge

Read the words of Psalm 23 aloud. Hear them and
hide them away in your heart.

EXPECTATIONS AND EXPECTING GOD

Day 2

Ask and it will be given to you; seek and you will find;
knock and the door will be opened to you.

SOMETIMES I HAVE unrealistic expectations. The vacation spot doesn't quite live up to the photos or reviews on the website. The cookies don't turn out quite like those perfect pictures. People don't give quite as much as they take.

Merriam-Webster defines *expectation* as "the act or state of expecting."[1] Okay, well, thanks for clearing that right up. Let's try the definition of "expect," then, shall we? To *expect* is "to consider probable or certain," or "to anticipate or look forward to the coming or occurrence of."[2] Yes, that's much more helpful.

What does all that have to do with God?

Recently, I've gotten into the habit of beginning each day with a verse. Before I ever get out of bed, I roll over, grab my phone, and open my Bible app. (I know experts say not to keep your phone next to your bed, but I'm guessing they don't have kids hours away at college or living on the other side of town.) As I read the verse of the day, I've come to expect God to gift me with just the right words of wisdom. Somehow, in a way only He could orchestrate, His words are always just what I need or just what I've been wanting to think about, even if I didn't know it yet.

Because God has so faithfully met with me for so many mornings, I am learning to expect Him. *To expect Him to meet me.* And, to my utter delight, I am discovering that—unlike those vacation spots, cookies, and draining

---

1 Merriam-Webster.com, s.v. "expectation (n.)," accessed December 13, 2022, *https://www.merriam-webster.com/dictionary/expectation.*

2 Merriam-Webster.com, s.v. "expect (v.)," accessed December 13, 2022, *https://www.merriam-webster.com/dictionary/expect.*

people—my expectations are not unrealistic. And they are not unmet. In fact, God faithfully meets with me in *all* the moments of my life—when I open my eyes to recognize His presence.

So, I'm cultivating a habit of seeking and searching for Him, of expecting Him and learning to expect Him. And as I seek out and search for Him, He meets my expectations again and again and again, far beyond anything I could ask for or imagine or expect . . . at every intersection of ordinary and divine.

Thank You, God, for always being found. Help my heart to never stop looking for You and to You. Amen.

Reflect

When we expect to find God in all the moments of our lives, He does not disappoint.

Read Matthew 7:7 and Jeremiah 29:13. What promises do these verses offer that we can expect God to keep? What is our role—according to these verses—in God's keeping of His promises?

_____

_____

_____

_____

_____

_____

_____

Where do you expect to see God? How can you cultivate a habit of seeking Him in all the moments of life?

_____

_____

_____

_____

_____

_____

_____

Challenge

Expect to see God today.

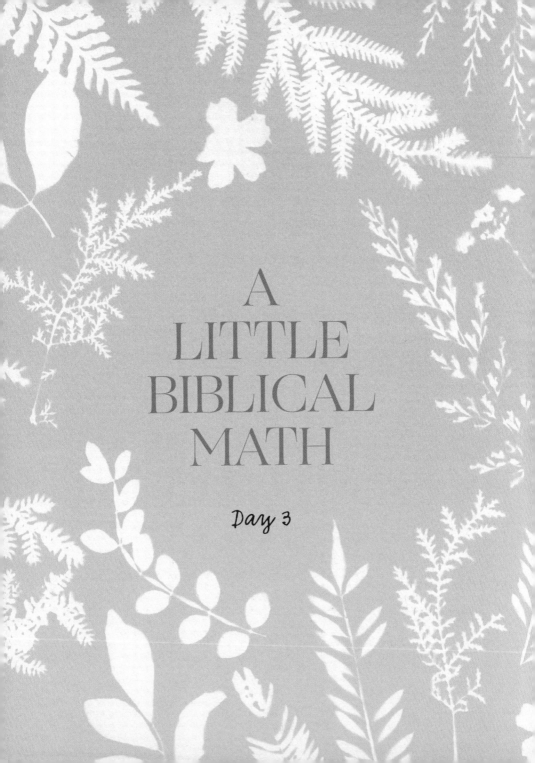

A LITTLE BIBLICAL MATH

Day 3

Take off your sandals, for the place where you
are standing is holy ground.

WHILE I SPEND MOST DAYS working with words, there's a part of me that loves math. Especially algebra. Crazy, right? (Although, when words and math join forces to create seemingly-impossible-to-solve problems about trains, speeds, and . . . Why are people taking my apples anyway? *That* I do not love.)

Perhaps it's the simple certainty of math that's so appealing. The way the numbers, letters, and unknowns resolve themselves into an orderly series of steps that lead straight to the one-and-only answer. I like one-and-only answers.

So it wasn't a complete surprise when, one day, I found myself studying a bit of Scripture—one I'd read a thousand times before—and suddenly applying a math formula to it.

If A equals B *and* B equals C, *then* A also equals C.

It's called the transitive law. I think.

The Scripture was Exodus 3. Moses had stepped up to the burning bush. (Because who wouldn't want a closer look at something like that?) Then the voice of God called out to him and said, "Take off your sandals, for the place where you are standing is holy ground."

Holy ground. Ground made holy by the presence of God.

Hold on to that thought and fast forward a few thousand years to the new covenant of Christ. As Jesus prepared to return to His Father, He promised a gift to us as believers: the Holy Spirit of God would come *to live inside us.* We would become His dwelling place (1 Corinthians 6:19). Which means that where we go, He goes. Every step of the way. So then . . . every step of the way becomes holy ground.

In other words:

If I am the dwelling place of God's presence *and* God's presence equals holy ground, *then* wherever I go is holy ground. Because He is with me.

Just a little beautiful, biblical math found at the intersection of ordinary and divine.

Lord, teach me to live as if every step is holy ground.

Reflect

Sit for a few moments in this bit of truth: As a follower of Christ, the Spirit of God is with you and within you. You are standing on holy ground.

What realizations—what reassurances—does the idea that you are forever standing on holy ground spark in you?

_____

_____

_____

_____

_____

_____

How does it impact your view of everyday life?

_____

_____

_____

_____

_____

_____

Challenge

Say His Name: _Lord, Father, Jesus, El Shaddai._ Then let yourself remember that He is here, with you, on this little patch of holy ground.

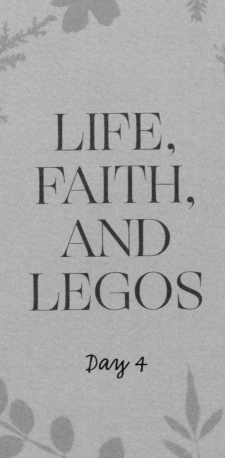

LIFE,
FAITH,
AND
LEGOS

Day 4

I have come that they may have life,
and have it to the full.

I LOVE LEGOS. I may or may not have bought Lego sets so that I could help my kids put them together. I may or may not still do this. Kids may or may not be involved. (No judgments here, right?)

There's something about the way Legos click and connect together that makes me smile. And then there's the way those piles of seemingly random little blocks—with all their odd shapes and sizes—join together to create something bigger. Something greater than all the pieces. Something with design and purpose. *Hmm.*

I'm starting to see that so much of life and faith and God—like those little Legos—comes down to connections. The more I read and study God's Word, the more connections I see. Old Testament to New Testament. Promises given and promises kept. And that "full," "rich and satisfying" (NLT) life that Jesus offers in John 10:10 with the words and mindset of Acts 17:28: "For in him we live and move and have our being."

I am convinced that the full, rich, and satisfying life is found only when we live and move and have our being in Christ. When we rise and sleep in Him, breathe and eat in Him, when each step, each movement is infused with an awareness of the presence of Him.

Even though those "big" mountaintop-moments of faith are wonderful and amazing, they don't happen every day. But embracing the living, moving, breathing moments of a life lived in connection with Him? This is possible every day.

I'm finding that when I do choose to live this way, those seemingly little random moments—with all their odd shapes and sizes—join together to create something bigger. Something greater than all the pieces. Something of His design, fulfilling His purpose in and for me.

Even in the smallest moments, here at the intersection of ordinary and divine.

Lord, teach me how to live a life more fully connected to You.

Reflect

Read John 15:1–17 and spend a few moments contemplating this idea of connection.

What would shift if you chose to *live and move and have your being* with an ongoing awareness of God's presence?

_____

_____

_____

_____

_____

_____

_____

In what everyday moments or objects do you see your connection to God?

_____

_____

_____

_____

_____

_____

_____

_____

Challenge

Look for connections today—like Legos—between life
and faith and God. What do you see?

EYES
THAT
SEE

Day 5

Blessed are your eyes because they see.

NOW THAT THE KIDS ARE OLDER, mornings find me tucked into a favorite "thinking" chair with a mug of something warm and God's Word open on my lap. It was there, one morning, that I once again came upon Matthew 13:16 and wondered—as I often have—over its phrasing: *Blessed are your eyes because they see.*

These words intrigue me. Because what else are eyes made to do but *see*? Could it be that *"seeing"* is about more than eyesight? Could it have less to do with my own myopic vision and more to do with my heart? Perhaps this kind of seeing is more about seeking and finding and trusting that the One who said He would always be with me really is here with me.

Are you like me? Do you struggle to see? Because there are days when, like Elisha's servant, I feel surrounded. Remember Elisha's servant? He's the one who awoke one morning to an army of enemies. They surrounded him, and the sight of them filled his eyes until enemies were all he could see (2 Kings 6:13–17).

I can relate. Too often, I am surrounded. By distractions and busyness. By worries and cares. And even, occasionally, by an enemy or two. (Thankfully, they aren't riding in chariots or carrying spears. Though that would make them easier to spot, wouldn't it?) Mostly, though, I am surrounded by the ordinary and everyday things of this world until those things are all I can see. In those moments, I need to lift up the words of Elisha—the prayer that enabled his servant to see the "hills full of horses and chariots of fire" (v. 17) all around him:

Lord, open my eyes to see.

It's a quiet prayer. Not fully voiced, but fully felt as I sit there in my chair . . . and it is answered. Transforming the old grandfather clock quietly tick-tocking time away into a reminder of the Father of All Time. That mama cardinal fluttering at the feeder whispers to me of the One who taught her to fly. And the puppy snoring softly at my feet? (*Beanie,* so named because he was the spitting image—and size—of those little Beanie Babies my kiddos collected once upon a time.) He's a fur-covered friend, gifted to me out of the infinite kindness of the One who chases away my loneliness.

If only I have eyes to see all the everyday blessings found here at the intersection of ordinary and divine.

Lord, open my eyes to see You.

Reflect

"Seeing" is seeking and finding and trusting
that the One who promised to be with you
really is right there.

What do your eyes see? Ask the Father to open your eyes, and then look again. What more do you see?

_____

_____

_____

_____

_____

_____

_____

Has there been a time when you glimpsed—with your eyes or with your heart—the presence of God?

_____

_____

_____

_____

_____

_____

_____

Challenge

Pray Elisha's prayer today and take note of all
that God opens your eyes to see.

LEAN IN TO LISTEN

Day 6

1 KING 19:12

After the earthquake came a fire, but the Lord was not
in the fire. And after the fire came a gentle whisper.

MY SON IS AN OLD SOUL. He notices. He ponders. And he asks questions.
The ones others rarely ask—at least not out loud. The ones that make me
think carefully and pray deeply before answering.

So, when he told me he was wrestling with a decision, I listened carefully. And when he told me he was seeking God's guidance, as a mama, I
rejoiced. But when he said he wasn't hearing God's answer, I began praying
for just the right words to encourage this old-soul son of mine.

My answer? It's one I've learned myself—the hard way, of course—in
those times when I myself have prayed and struggled to hear God's leading:
God always answers, but He doesn't often shout. Instead, He whispers. Why?
So that we'll lean in closer to listen.

Over time, as my son and I both kept seeking and praying—as we leaned
in to listen—God's answer did become clear. And another stone was laid in
the foundation of my son's faith.

Surprisingly, this whole conversation—and most of the follow-up
ones—happened through a chain of text messages. Because my son is away
at college, and that's the way so much of our communication happens these
days.

I have a bit of a love-hate relationship with texting. As a writer, I am
more than a little obsessed with all the spelling, punctuation, and paragraph
things. (And don't even talk to me about autocorrect.) I need the richness
of actual conversations shared over cups of something warm and plates of
something chocolate, or salty, or both. Texting, by contrast, seems shallow
and coldly convenient.

Until it isn't.

When we bathe our words in prayer, when we use them to encourage ourselves and others to lean in closer to God, it doesn't matter how they are shared. And not even autocorrect can dim that connection between ordinary and divine.

Lord, fill me with Your truth, Your wisdom, and Your words as I lean in to listen to You.

Reflect

Because God is always with and within us,
we are surrounded by the whispers of His truth.
Be still, lean in, and listen.

Why do you believe God so often whispers instead of shouting out His answers? Write of a time God whispered to you.

_____

_____

_____

_____

_____

_____

_____

Are you seeking an answer from God? How might you lean into Him as you wait for His response?

_____

_____

_____

_____

_____

Challenge

Use your words today—face-to-face, over the phone, or in a text—to encourage someone to lean in closer and listen to God's whispers.

EVEN IN THE ICKY

Day 7

PSALM 37:23 NLT

The LORD directs the steps of the godly.
He delights in every detail of their lives.

SHIMMERING. IT'S NOT A WORD WE OFTEN USE in our everyday vocabulary. I'm thinking I should use it more. Along with *gossamer, silken,* and *ephemeral.* What has this thesaurus strolling through my thoughts? A spider's web. Strong as steel and fleeting as the dew.

A wisp of a spider's web waves in the wind outside my kitchen window. The sight of it shimmering in the morning rays sends me scrambling for a pencil to capture my thoughts before they melt away.

But ordinary words cannot capture this extraordinary wisp of a thing.

Please understand—I am not a huge fan of spiders. I'm not even a little fan of spiders. I suppose it comes from having lived in a near–century-old house of stone where spiders appeared often and without warning. Creeping and peeping in and out of cracks in the old tongue-and-groove wood panels. (Insert shiver here.)

But spider *webs*—even this wisp of a web outside my window—fascinate and delight me.

According to scientists, if steel could be spun to the thickness of a spider's web, the web would be the stronger of the two. And then there's the intricacy of their designs, the deadly cleverness of their weavings. Each species' web is perfectly suited to a unique purpose—whether catching and wrapping up prey, lining nests, or even creating parachutes for eight-legged wind travelers.

Icky, but amazing.

Because the same God Who created mountains and moons and majestic heights also gave the little spider its web. E. B. White's Charlotte might have woven words into her webs, but God weaves thoughtfulness into His designs. A thoughtfulness that extends right down into the details of my life. Nothing is deemed too small or insignificant to escape His care.

Not even this wisp of a spider's web waving outside my window, reminding me of the connection between ordinary and divine.

Lord, I praise You for
being a God who works
in even the tiniest details
of my life.

Reflect

Our God is big enough to create an infinite
universe and fill it with untold wonders, yet He is
thoughtful and loving enough to be present and
working in even the tiniest details of our lives.

Where do you see the vastness of God? Where do you see His thoughtfulness and attention to detail?

_____

_____

_____

_____

_____

_____

_____

How do these two facets of God—His vastness and His attention to detail—impact your view of Him? Of your life and faith?

_____

_____

_____

_____

_____

_____

_____

Challenge

Search out a spider's web. What do you *really* see?

CREATING
JOY

Day 8

Take delight in the Lord,
and he will give you the desires of your heart.

YOU MIGHT THINK I'M A BIT SILLY, or even strange—and you wouldn't be the first—but on my kitchen counter sits a bottle of bubbles. Not bubbles that scrub. Not even bubble bath for relaxing. Just an old-fashioned, entertain-the-littles-with-it bottle of bubbles. The kind with the little plastic wand tucked inside. But they're not for the littles. They're mine. (Insert smiley face here.)

As you are no doubt aware, some days are filled with wonder and delight. Other days have moments of delight sprinkled in. And then there are *those* days. When the task list is relentless, when one thing after another goes wrong, when plans go awry, and when feelings are hurt. Days when we need a bit of joy to tide us over and get us through. But the joy is in short supply.

On those days, I've learned that I sometimes need to create my own joy. Hence the bubbles. Why bubbles? Because they never fail to make me smile. And because they never fail to make me ponder once again the questions of childhood.

Why are bubbles round?

How do they float?

Where do all the colors come from?

The questions remind me that, while I may be the one sitting here blowing the bubbles, it's God who made the physics, or chemistry, or whatever it is that makes bubbles possible. It's God who is the Creator of joy. And it's His Spirit within me that has me seeking out His wonders.

Bubbles might not do the trick for you. Instead, it might be the swing of a golf club or the thwack of a racket hitting the ball. It might be riding your bike downhill—no feet on the pedals, the smell of cookies pulled fresh from the oven, or any number of other things that connect you to the simple joys of life.

Whatever they might look like for you, these little respites from life allow us to refocus, resettle, and relegate the cares of this world to His more-than-capable hands. And it's these simple joys that help us find our way back to the intersection of ordinary and divine.

Lord, when joy is in short supply, remind me to seek and take delight in You. Amen.

What simple delights make you smile and help you recenter your thoughts on God when the world has knocked your day askew? What keeps you from "indulging" in the simple joys?

_____

_____

_____

_____

_____

_____

_____

God is not only the creator of joy, but the One who offers you an eternity of joy. Write out a prayer inviting God into this moment and asking Him to reveal His joy to you.

_____

_____

_____

_____

_____

Challenge

Indulge in something that brings you delight. Create a
bit of joy and thank God for the reason to smile.

SWEETER
THAN
HONEY

Day 9

How sweet your words taste to me;
they are sweeter than honey.

THERE'S NOTHING QUITE LIKE wrapping your fingers around a mug of hot tea on a cold day. And a generous spoonful of honey stirred in gives it just the right touch of sweetness.

I have a special affection for honey. (Would it be too much of a pun to say that I have *sweet* memories of honey? Yeah, I thought so.) I suppose it goes back to when my grandfather was alive and kept bees. On the days he "robbed" the hives, he'd let me pick out bits of chewy comb dripping with fresh honey. It was always such a sweet and sticky treat.

Which brings me to the one problem with honey: its stickiness. Just a drop spilled from my spoon or dribbled down the side of the honey jar can "stickify" an entire acre of my kitchen. ("Stickify" might not appear in the dictionary, but it is a much-used word around our house.)

As I was swiping up just such a drip of honey this afternoon, I happened to think of that verse about God's Word being sweeter than honey. Psalm 119:103. (I had to go and look it up. Am I the only one who can't seem to remember verse numbers?) As I kept swiping at that stickiness on my mug, my fingers, and now half of the kitchen island, I wondered if there might be a sort of double meaning in the verse that refers not only to the sweetness of God's Word but also to its stickiness. In Isaiah 55:11, God tells us that "[His Word] will not return to me empty, but will accomplish what I desire and achieve the purpose for which I sent it." In other words, it will *stick* until it has done what He sent it to do.

What does God's Word do? It equips (2 Timothy 3:16–17), protects (Ephesians 6:17), and sanctifies (John 17:17). It is truth (Proverbs 30:5) and light (Psalm 119:105) and life (Matthew 4:4) to all who savor its sweetness.

Just a sweet little truth stuck there at the intersection of ordinary and divine.

Lord, thank You for sweetening my life with Your Word.

Reflect

The Word of God is sweeter—and stickier— than honey.

How or when has the Word of God stuck with you?

_____

_____

_____

_____

_____

Search the Bible for verses about the Word of God. What other truths do you find?

_____

_____

_____

_____

_____

_____

_____

Memorizing Scripture is one of the best ways to savor the sweetness of God's Word. Choose a verse to memorize and write it here.

_____

_____

_____

_____

_____

_____

_____

_____

======= *Challenge* =======

Slip away with the Bible—and perhaps a cup
of honey-sweetened tea—and savor the sweetness
of God's Word.

CONVERSATIONS
WITHOUT END

Day 10

Pray without ceasing.

I ONCE THOUGHT THAT "AMEN" was a sort of combination between "the end" and the stamp on a letter. That it said both, "That's all for now" and "Here you go, Lord." That those four little letters had the power to close my prayer and send it on its way, propelling it up to heaven and into the presence of God. So I thought.

I will confess that I was much older than a child when I put away such beliefs.

I will also confess that the saddest part wasn't that I believed *amen* sent my prayers on their way. Rather, it was that I believed—or at least, acted as if I believed—that it closed the conversation with God and allowed me to let my thoughts roam unhindered by His overhearing.

I know better now. More importantly, I *do* better now.

Amen isn't a stamp, a seal, or even "the end." According to Strong's, it means *truly* or *so be it*.[1] It is an echo of the ending of Jesus's own prayers to His Father: "Your will be done" (Matthew 6:10, Matthew 26:42). Instead of marking the end of a conversation, it represents the transition to a new beginning. A switch to a different sort of prayer. To a prayer without end.

That continued conversation, those here-and-there whispers scattered throughout the day, are, I believe, the essence of Paul's command to "pray without ceasing." For as I seek to step into agreement with God—*so be it, Father*—the conversation continues.

---

1 "H543—'Āmēn—Strong's Hebrew Lexicon (Kjv)," Blue Letter Bible, accessed January 13, 2023, https://www.blueletterbible.org/lexicon/h543/kjv/wlc/0-1/.

Sometimes I am actively participating, whether through speaking or listening, as I turn the events of the day over to His care and concern. Other times, my mind is filled with the tasks and busyness of life. Yet, even after the amen, the conversation—the communication—continues on without words, within me and all around me as I remain fully aware of His presence. Fully aware and with a heart continually surrendered to Him.

May His will be done, here at the intersection of ordinary and divine.

So be it. Your will be done. Amen and amen.

Reflect

As you finish this day's prayer and whisper "amen," be reminded that it's not the end of the conversation; it's the beginning.

Have you ever treated *amen* as a postage stamp, sealing your prayer and sending it on its way? Checking that "item" off your to-do list for today? If so, how would you like your prayers to be?

_____

_____

_____

_____

_____

Today, practice allowing *amen* to be the beginning of your conversation with God rather than the end. Tomorrow, return here and record your thoughts about this practice and how it impacted your thoughts and your day.

_____

_____

_____

_____

_____

_____

_____

Challenge

Scatter whispers of *amen, so be it,*
and *Your will be done* throughout your day—
and notice the difference it makes.

TRAVELING SLOWLY

Day 11

Come to me, all you who are weary and burdened,
and I will give you rest.

I ONCE HEARD A SPEAKER USE the analogy of a racecar to describe a life of faith. He wanted to zoom along the roads of life as fast as he could, doing all he possibly could for the Lord, and arrive in heaven with a screech of tires and a sideways drift, completely used up, emptied out, and out of gas.

His words stole my breath—and not in a good way. Oh, I loved the middle part about doing all I could for the Lord, but the bookends of that scenario? The zooming through life at top speed and screeching into heaven, used up, emptied out, and out of gas? Well, honestly, that visual made me a little queasy. I'm not a zooming, rushing, screeching sort of person. I could be the poster child for introverted, bookish nerd. And I like me that way.

But when I heard that analogy, I was at a point in my faith when I soaked up everyone else's ideas and believed I needed to apply them to my own life. I have since learned better. (Mostly.) I realize now that God created each of us with different strengths and that we need to play to those. Racecar driving is not my strength. I prefer to take my time.

So that whole racecar way of life? No, thank you. There's quite enough racing through this life as it is, so I'll leave the speedy lifestyle to those who love zooming and screeching. Yes, I plan to wring out of life all it has to offer, but instead of a racecar, I think I'd like a wagon—like one of those that Laura Ingalls rode in across the prairies. A wagon hitched to a sweet, steadily moving horse. Traveling slowly, so that I can savor both the moments and each person I meet along the way. I'd want a wagon big enough to carry the wounded and those too weary to walk. I'd toss in cozy blankets to soften the bumps and allow for conversation and companionship. And I'd make sure we had plenty of time to stop and admire the view at every intersection of ordinary and divine.

Lord, whether I'm traveling slowly or zooming through this day, let all that I do be done for You. Amen.

Reflect

Whether we travel through life in a racecar,
a wagon, or something in between, what matters
is that our journey takes us—and others—
closer and closer to God.

Imagine life as a road you are traveling on your way to heaven. What are you riding in? How fast are you going? Who is with you? Is there room for others or time to stop along the way? Would you like to change the way you're traveling?

_____

_____

_____

_____

_____

_____

_____

Do you ever feel pressured to adopt other people's approach to faith? Why do you think that is?

_____

_____

_____

_____

_____

_____

Challenge

Search the Bible for a time when Jesus ran.
Ponder what you do—or don't—find.

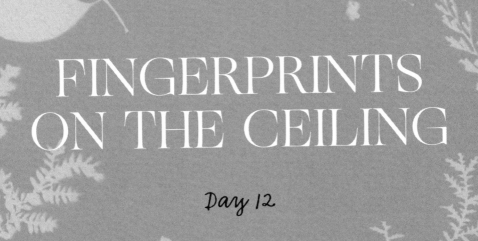

FINGERPRINTS ON THE CEILING

Day 12

For since the creation of the world God's invisible
qualities—his eternal power and divine nature—have
been clearly seen, being understood from what has
been made, so that people are without excuse.

ON THE OCCASIONS WHEN I REMEMBER TO DUST, I find fingerprints in the strangest places. Of course, there are fingerprints on the windows and the sliding glass door. Fingerprints on the refrigerator and microwave. Fingerprints on the doorways, as well as the doors. But the ceiling? I have to admit it was a bit of a surprise to look up and see that, yes, there are in fact fingerprints on my ceiling. Left there, no doubt, by my 6′5″ and still-growing son who loves to see how far—or rather, how *not* far—he has to stretch up to touch said ceiling. (There are also some smudges that look suspiciously like footprints, but I'm not going to ask too many questions about how those got there.)

I guess I should try to clean those fingerprints off or perhaps paint over them, but now that my son is off to college more than he is home, I find myself thinking rather fondly of those fingerprints. They are a reminder of His presence. And they make me smile. (Sometimes ruefully. But smile nevertheless.)

Something similar happens when I step outside into nature. I see fingerprints everywhere. Not the fingerprints of my children. But the fingerprints of God. The fingerprints of His sovereignty as Lord of all that is seen and unseen (Colossians 1:16). The fingerprints of His imagination in all the many shapes and sizes and colors of trees (Genesis 1:11). And, yes, even the fingerprints of His faithfulness on the ceiling of heaven through each rising and setting of the Sun (Jeremiah 31:35). All these fingerprints have been left there by God for us to find. To point to Him as Creator. To give us reasons to trust and to believe.

Each time I step into His creation, I am reminded that if He can make an ocean, a flower, and a tree, and if He can count the stars and the grains of sand and the hairs upon my head, then He is surely able to take care of me as I walk with Him through all the intersections of ordinary and divine.

Lord, slow my steps this day to see and savor the fingerprints of Your creation all around me. Amen.

Reflect

We are surrounded by the evidence—
the fingerprints—of God.

Step outside and watch the sunset this evening. Describe what you see. What does the setting sun tell you about the nature of God?

_____

_____

_____

_____

_____

_____

Where do you most vividly see evidences of God? How do they strengthen your belief in His goodness?

_____

_____

_____

_____

_____

_____

Challenge

Watch the sunrise each morning for a week—and begin your day in awe of the power and creativity of God.

TURTLE SHELLS AND FORTRESSES

Day 13

The Lord is my rock, my fortress, and my deliverer;
my God is my rock, in whom I take refuge.

OCCASIONALLY, WE FIND TURTLES AROUND OUR HOUSE. (Outside, not inside—thank goodness!) Sometimes they're out near the road, as if they've been traveling and just stopped by for a visit. Other times, one will appear under the trees or out in the yard. They're little box turtles. And these water-loving guys are clearly lost.

I worry most about those we find on the road. I'm not a particularly brave person when it comes to wildlife, but my concern gives me courage. I can pick up a little lost turtle—whose toes I fear will burn on the summer-hot asphalt of our street—and put it in the shade of a tree or the cool of the grass—safely out of reach of any passing cars.

Inevitably, when I rescue a turtle, it's terrified. It tucks inside its shell, and no amount of coaxing can induce it to show so much as its tiny turtle nose or toes.

There are moments when I wish I could do the same—tuck my head in and block out my surroundings. Or even find a fortress to duck into. Because hiding away from the world sounds particularly good on some days, especially when certain dangers—or uncomfortable situations—come to town.

But then . . . I *have* a fortress, don't I? In fact, as children of God, we all do. It's the fortress of God's love and promised protection.

For a long time, I believed that *fortress* was the place to run to when I felt threatened or overwhelmed. Then I realized one day—with sudden, almost shocking clarity—that the fortress of God isn't something to run to; it's something that surrounds me always. In other words . . .

God is more than a refuge I can run to. He is the fortress where I can live!

And that changes so many things, doesn't it?

I don't have to shrink back from the challenges—or even dangers—of this world. I can be brave and bold, because I live every moment surrounded by the fortress of God's love, presence, and protection.

Now, *that* is an intersection of ordinary and divine!

Lord, open my heart and mind to the reality of the ever–present fortress of Your Presence. Amen.

Reflect

As a child of God, you can *live* in the fortress of God's love, presence, and protection.

Have you been thinking of God as Someone you have to run to? What does it mean to know that He's already here with you?

_____

_____

_____

_____

Does knowing that the fortress of God always surrounds you change your view of the challenges and dangers of living in this world?

_____

_____

_____

_____

How might knowing that the fortress of God's love, presence, and protection is always with you help you to be brave? To do what you need to do?

_____

_____

_____

_____

Challenge

When life throws one of its challenges at you,
remember you are surrounded by the fortress of God.

MAKING
ROOM

Day 14

There is more than enough room in my Father's home.

DO YOU EVER FEEL AS THOUGH you're in a perpetual state of clearing out? I'm there with you. My house is constantly getting cluttered with stuff, especially in the closets. I think the stuff in there multiplies every time I close the door.

In truth, it's my own fault. I have a tendency to rush in to put something away and then stash it wherever it fits. Or I save a box because it's a really good box—and I might need it one day. That same kind of "someday" thinking has resulted in bins of baby clothes I can't bear to part with stacked next to boxes of pictures I plan to organize.

Every few months, I do manage to clean out and sort through the stuff, just to keep the chaos under some semblance of control. I recycle a few not-quite-so-good boxes and tidy away the stashed stuff to its rightful place. The clearing out makes room for the things that matter.

I find that I need to do the same thing with my time now and then. I need to clear out a few things I thought I needed but really don't. And I need to let go of those things that simply aren't needed anymore to make room for what really matters. To make room for God.

Because, for me, it's so easy to allow the rush and jumble of days to steal the space I've cleared out for God. When He calls to me, I too often duck my head and hear myself mumbling, *I'll do that later,* knowing full well that *later* hardly ever comes. Which is crazy, because He is the One who equips me with all the love, strength, and joy I need to make it through a day in this world in the first place.

Though I sometimes struggle to make room for Him, that is not a struggle God shares. He is forever faithful, never failing to make room at His table (Luke 13:29), in His family (1 John 3:1), and in His kingdom (Luke 12:32). He's got a spot waiting just for me—and for you—at the intersection of ordinary and divine.

Lord, teach my heart to make room for You. Amen.

Reflect

God always has a place for you in His presence.

We might sometimes experience times and places in our lives where there is no room for us. No room at the table, at the party, or in the meeting. What does it mean to you that God always has room for you?

_____

_____

_____

_____

_____

_____

Our days and our lives always go so much better after time spent with God. Why, then, do you think, is it such a challenge to carve out that time for Him?

_____

_____

_____

_____

_____

_____

Challenge

Examine your days. What unnecessary things can
you clear away to make more room for God?

MESSY,
BUT
DIVINE

Day 15

He fills my life with good things.

I HAVE A CONFESSION TO MAKE. I live in a family of droppers—and I am their queen. Yes, I am the droppiest dropper of them all.

What's a dropper? It's someone who drops whatever item is in hand, wherever they happen to be standing. (That would be me and mine.) The kitchen table is our most frequent dropping spot. Receipts, bits of mail, pocket change, car keys, and things we mustn't forget. It can create quite a mess. Oddly enough, the kitchen table is where I'm actually *supposed* to drop my glasses, but that has fifty-fifty odds at best.

Our family's dropping habit is a constant source of irritation for me, but since a healthy share of the dropped stuff is mine, I must keep my frustration to myself. Mostly.

Despite the mess, all those dropped things do remind me of some wonderful truths. First, they remind me that my home is filled with people I love and activities that make up our daily lives. They also remind me of the God Who has promised He will not only never drop me (Isaiah 41:10), but also will never allow anyone or anything to snatch me from His hand (John 10:27–29). Those dropped things also remind me that—unlike the stuff on our kitchen table—God won't leave me however I've happened to land (2 Corinthians 3:18). Instead, He's constantly working on me and in me, shaping me to be more and more like His Son.

And finally, all those little dropped things remind me that God is something of a dropper Himself. He drops verses into my thoughts to guide and inspire me. He drops people into my path to help me and be helped by me. And He drops moments of joy and gifts of wonder into my day for me to discover.

Yes, life—and my kitchen table—can get messy. But it's a divine mess filled with souvenirs from the intersection of ordinary and divine.

Lord, help me to search out the joys You drop into each day. Amen.

Reflect

God drops moments of joy and gifts of wonder into all the moments of our lives.

How can life be both messy and divine? Where do you see the divine "dropping" into your mess?

_____

_____

_____

_____

_____

God will never drop you or allow you to be snatched away. What reassurance does this give you?

_____

_____

_____

_____

_____

_____

Challenge

How many souvenirs from the intersection of ordinary
and divine can you find in your day?

LISTS
AND
PLANS

Day 16

PROVERBS 16:9 NLT

We can make our plans,
but the LORD determines our steps.

EVERY MORNING I SIT AT THE BREAKFAST TABLE and make my to-do list. It's usually very specific, since I like checking things off a list. Every scratched-through item makes me feel as if I've accomplished something. My list usually has far more items on it than anyone could ever hope to conquer in a single twenty-four hours, but having the list in hand lends structure to my day. And there's a certain comfort in knowing the plans I have for myself.

All my careful planning and plotting probably gives God a chuckle every morning as He sees me ordering my steps. Because of course, He knows my days better than I do and will most likely turn them in a far different direction than I expect. Reshaping my plan to fit His own perfect one.

I don't know about your house, but detours, delays, and interruptions are a way of life around ours. And while not every interruption is a divine one, each seems to offer up some sort of divine opportunity to share His mercy, grace, and love. But only if I have the eyes and the heart—and the good sense—to recognize it.

As I've been reading through the Gospels again, I've noticed how often Jesus's plans were detoured, delayed, and interrupted. Whether by those needing help and healing, by those needing answers, or by those needing to justify their own wayward ways. I'm also realizing how often *I* interrupt Jesus. Sometimes with prayer and praise, but much more often with pleas for help and healing, for answers, and for mercy and grace when I try to justify my own wayward ways.

Personally? I'm so grateful Jesus chooses to handle my interruptions the way He handled all those long-ago detours and delays—with love and kindness, with truth, and by always pointing back to the Father. His responses challenge me to approach the changes to my day's plans in the same way. To view them not as annoyances, but as opportunities to show love and kindness, to share truth, and to point others back to the Father. In other words, to play a small part in helping others find the intersection of ordinary and divine.

Lord, thank You for
always greeting me and
my interruptions with
love and grace. Amen.

Reflect

Every detour, delay, and interruption brings
with it a divine opportunity to show and
share the Father's love.

How do you tend to view detours, delays, and interruptions to your day?

_____

_____

_____

_____

_____

_____

Do you ever think God might chuckle a bit over your to-do list? Pen a prayer here, surrendering your list to Him.

_____

_____

_____

_____

_____

_____

_____

Challenge

Interrupt Jesus today with prayer and praise.

WOVEN
ALL
THROUGH

Day 17

For you created my inmost being;
you knit me together in my mother's womb.

I TAUGHT MY DAUGHTER TO CROCHET, just as my grandmothers taught me. Stitch by stitch. Simple patterns and simple, straight lines.

She quickly left me in the dust.

Thread flows through her fingers like water, creating lacey shawls with patterned images of Victorian ladies gathering flowers in a garden—all intricate designs that make my eyes twitch. Blankets practically drip from her fingers. She even taught herself to knit, using four needles at once to create the tiniest baby cardigans with impossibly tiny, seamless sleeves. (I'm sticking to crochet—only one needle.)

I am in awe.

As I admire the intricate stitches, I am amazed at my daughter's undeniable attention to detail. The care for her creation is woven into each and every stitch. And whenever she begins stitching together some new project, I can't help but think of the words from Psalm 139: *You knit me together in my mother's womb.*

Knit together.

Thoughtfully planned out and so carefully handcrafted. Stitch by loving stitch.

If you've ever so much as sewn a button onto a shirt, you have an inkling of just what this entails.

In the same way, the Father's touch is on every stitch of our being. Every cell, every strand of hair, every bit of DNA. Thoughtfully planned out before even one of our days came to be. Fearfully and marvelously crafted by His hands. His works are wonderful, *that* we can know full well (Psalm 139:14).

Just as the power and plans of God are woven all throughout our bodies, He invites us to weave His power and presence, with that same attention to detail, into every aspect of our lives. Into our thoughts. Our hearts and souls. Our eternities. It's an invitation I joyfully and so gratefully accept, because God is the thread Who holds me together and binds everything I do—everything I am—to Him.

So when I see those stitches flying from my daughter's fingers, I am reminded of all the wonderful details just waiting for me to discover at this intersection of ordinary and divine.

Oh Lord, I praise You for the way You have made me, and for the way You have made me *Yours*. Amen.

Reflect

Every cell, every strand of hair, and every bit of DNA was carefully and thoughtfully crafted together to create you.

What does it mean to you to be knit together by God? Does knowing this affect how you see yourself? How you view other people's opinions of you? And does it affect how you see others, who are also knit together by Him?

_____

_____

_____

_____

_____

_____

What changes when you accept God's invitation and allow His power and presence to be woven into every moment and every aspect of your life? How do these changes create intersections of ordinary and divine?

_____

_____

_____

_____

_____

Challenge

Look in the mirror today and give yourself
a smile—because you are fearfully, wonderfully,
and marvelously knit together by God, and He
has good plans for you.

CLOTHES
AND
CLOTHS

Day 18

LUKE 2:7

She wrapped him in cloths and placed him in a manger.

THIS MIGHT SOUND A BIT CRAZY, but I've always found something satisfying about folding clothes. (*Clothes* or *cloths*? I always have to check!) Especially towels. Now, I'm not saying I get to the folding as soon as the dryer sings its "I'm all done" song. But when I do get around to the folding, I find it to be soothing. And I'm not even being the least bit sarcastic here.

Perhaps it's the joy of seeing the jumbled, tumbled chaos being sorted into neat and orderly piles. Or perhaps it's the visible reminder that there is one job I can actually finish. At least for the 30.7 seconds before the next load of laundry needs to be done. (Save me.)

But as I was folding laundry the other day, the thoughts tumbling through my mind were not about *clothes* but about *cloths*. (I double-checked the spellings!) I thought of the cloths in Luke 2:7 that Mary wrapped around her newborn son—God's Son. I thought of the servant's cloth Jesus wrapped around His waist as He knelt to wash the feet of His disciples. The same feet that, just a few hours later, would run away from Him (John 13:3–5). And I also thought about the cloth that covered the head of Jesus as He lay in the grave. The one that was neatly folded and laid aside when He rose up and left that tomb empty (John 20:7).

Swaddling cloths. A servant's cloth. Grave cloths.

Just simple, ordinary pieces of fabric, but these cloths represent so much more in my life and in my faith. The beautiful beginning of a baby, the Son born of God. The beautiful example of the servant's life I am to lead. And those grave cloths? They're not an ending. They represent yet another beginning, made possible by the love and sacrifice of Christ. A beginning even more wonderful than that long-ago, swaddled-up-in-Bethlehem one.

Clothes and *cloths.* Just one more glimpse of that miraculous intersection of ordinary and divine.

Lord, I thank You for these little reminders of all You have given to and for me. Amen.

Reflect

Three cloths—swaddling, a servant's, and grave—bundle up the life, example, and sacrifice of Jesus.

Jesus needed both swaddling cloths and grave cloths. What does that reveal about the Son of God who was also the Son of Man? And what does that servant's cloth tell you about why He came?

_____

_____

_____

_____

_____

_____

As you go about your ordinary tasks and chores, look for ways that they remind you of God and His Son. What do you find?

_____

_____

_____

_____

_____

_____

_____

Challenge

As you fold that next load of clothes,
allow your thoughts to wander back to those
three cloths in the life of Jesus.

WONDERING
AND
WANDERING

Day 19

For the Son of Man came to seek and to save the lost.

DO YOU EVER WONDER? I do. I'm a wonderer. About anything and every-thing. My thoughts sometimes take more twists and turns than a Tennessee mountain backroad. And speaking of twisty roads, I'm also a wanderer. (The two might be connected.) My family will attest to the fact that I have absolutely no sense of direction.

Here's a replay of one conversation with my son, which took place as I made yet another lap around the same block:

"Are you lost?" he asked.

My reply? "Of course not. I'm just not quite sure where I am."

In my mind, *lost* means hopeless and on the verge of tears (been there and done that). Whereas not knowing where I am means that I still believe I can find my way back to something familiar. Eventually.

In my defense, Nashville is a maze of one-way roads and streets that have the same name—like Old Hickory Boulevard that stretches across the city in fits and starts but is in no way fully connected. (Also, when I was in my twenties, the city decided it would be a good idea to change the names of the interstates that thread through it, and I've never quite recovered.) So believe me when I say I am quite familiar with the bit of panic involved in getting lost. And with the joy-filled relief of being found.

Of course, this idea of being lost and found applies on the roads, yes, but even more so in life and faith. Because though I wonder and sometimes question why, and though I mess up and often wander from the path God has laid out before me, I know that He will not rest until I am found. Because He is the One who seeks and saves the lost (Luke 19:10). He doesn't stand idly by. Instead, He chases after (Psalm 23:6), scoops up (Luke 15:5), and welcomes the wondering and the wandering back to Him (Luke 15:20).

So, yes, sometimes I wonder and even wander, but I trust God to always lead me back to Him at the intersection of ordinary and divine.

Lord, thank You for listening to my wonderings and for guiding my wanderings always back to You. Amen.

Reflect

God does not shy away from our wonderings, and He does not leave us lost in our wanderings.

Have you ever been well and truly lost? How did that feel? Describe the joy and relief of being found.

_____

_____

_____

_____

Read Luke 15. What do these stories of being lost and found say about God and His desire for a relationship with you?

_____

_____

_____

_____

_____

_____

God doesn't turn away from our questions (just check out some of David's questions in the Psalms). What wonderings would you like to ask God?

_____

_____

_____

_____

_____

_____

_____

Challenge

Go wandering—through the city, the park,
or your own backyard. While you wander,
talk to God about your wonderings.

STARRY
NIGHTS

Day 20

He counts the stars
and calls them all by name.

DON'T TELL MY HUSBAND, but I kind of enjoy that last late-night walk with our puppy Beanie around the cul-de-sac. (Unless it's raining, of course. Or really cold.) In spite of the noises of the nearby city, the world at night is hushed and the darkness wraps around me like a quilt. Coyotes howl in the distance, while the glow of eyes peers out at me from the backyard as the neighborhood deer settle in for the night.

As Beanie and I walk along, I gaze up at the stars, twinkling in the sky like summertime's fireflies. (I'm actually writing these thoughts in winter, and every night I search for the flash of a shooting star from the Geminids meteor shower.) Because I'm out here every night, I watch the Moon shine through its phases, waxing and waning and waxing again. I stop for a moment, my feet rooted in place. I can almost feel the spin of the Earth as it circles around and around in a solar system that, in turn, circles around and around the Milky Way.

On these nights, I am overcome by the sheer vastness and perfection and wonder of God's creation. How is all this that I see even possible?

The answer, of course, is God. He is the one Who holds this whole world in His hands, Who keeps it suspended in the nothingness of space (Job 26:7). It is He Who stacked up the mountains and scooped out the seas. And it was His word that flew across the emptiness of space, creating light and life and everything in between (Genesis 1, Psalm 33:6).

In the same way, it is by His mercy that I stand here, staring up at these stars that only He can count.

It is by His grace that I will one day see the face of the One Who calls them all by name. And it is because of His love that I will hear Him call my name.

Until then, I will meet with Him each night, at this star-filled intersection of ordinary and divine.

Lord, thank You for
Your mercy, Your grace,
and a love so great that
You know my name.
Amen.

Reflect

The One Who counts and calls the stars by name
also knows and calls your name.

Search online for some of the latest images sent back by the Hubble Space Telescope or the James Webb Space Telescope. What thoughts do these pictures inspire?

_____

_____

_____

_____

_____

_____

God is vast enough to know every detail of a universe we haven't even been able to measure. And He is intimate enough to know the hairs on your head (Matthew 10:29–31) and each day of your life (Psalm 139:16). What does that tell you about God? His power? His mercy, grace, and love?

_____

_____

_____

_____

_____

_____

Challenge

Take a walk under the stars. (The puppy is optional, but highly recommended.)

MORE
THAN
BOOKS
CAN
HOLD

Day 21

Jesus did many other things as well. If every one
of them were written down, I suppose that even
the whole world would not have room for the books
that would be written.

I HAVE ALWAYS DREAMED of having my own library. One recent summer, that dream came true when I built my own. Okay, maybe *built* isn't quite accurate. I *assembled* it. With a lot of help from Ikea and online tutorials. Regardless of how skilled (or unskilled) the process, I absolutely adore the results. I now have enough walls wrapped in bookshelves to confidently claim that I have my own little library.

Do you think there will be libraries and stacks of books in heaven? I'm hoping there are. (I'm also hoping for a gigantic movie screen where I can watch all the events of creation and the Bible unfold before my eyes, so that all my questions about dinosaurs and Nephilim and the parting of the Red Sea can be answered!) But if there aren't books in heaven (or giant movie screens), that can only mean one thing: there's something even better. (Of course, the greatest thing will be seeing God!)

Ever since I learned to read, books have been both my refuge and my respite. Hiding away in a hammock of branches in our old backyard tree was my favorite way to read. From there, I traveled the prairies with Laura, untangled mysteries with Nancy Drew, and reveled in the shipwreck adventures of *The Swiss Family Robinson*. In many ways, it was reading that led me to God and His Word. But that's another story.

As an incurable (and unrepentant) bibliophile, I'll never forget the thrill I felt after first stumbling across John 21:25. Imagine: so much wonder and so many words that not even the whole world could contain the books needed to tell all that Jesus has done. I can't help but wonder if those books have been written and are waiting for me—for all of us—to read one day *with Him.*

Until then, I'll have to be content with my own little library. It's a lovely spot, filled with books and words, each a reminder of the many different intersections of ordinary and divine.

Lord, thank You for
all the wonders found
in Your word—and all
the wonders You're
still writing in my life!
Amen.

Reflect

If the whole world were filled with books, it still
could not contain all the wonders of Jesus.

In many ways, books led me to God and His Word. What led you to Him?

_____

_____

_____

_____

_____

_____

John 21:25 makes me wonder what heaven will be like. What verse prompts you to wonder about heaven? What questions do you hope will be answered in heaven?

_____

_____

_____

_____

_____

_____

Challenge

Choose a book from the Bible and begin reading
it today—to learn from, yes, but also simply to enjoy
the presence of God within the pages.

A
MINISTRY
OF
MOMENTS

Day 22

EPHESIANS 5:16 NCV

Use every chance you have for doing good.

MY DAUGHTER IS ALL GROWN UP NOW and creating a home of her own. As I watch her making her way and doing all the grown-up things—like paying taxes (Who said FICA could take so much money?) and trying out new recipes, the memories of her childhood flood my mind. And I'm realizing a few things.

First, our family has experienced lots of big moments together. Moments of adventure as we explored new places and things. Moments of honors and awards. And, yes, moments of faith.

We crammed *a lot* of life into those big moments. But as I step back to watch my daughter growing into who she is created to be, I realize that the bulk of our lives was not in those big moments. It was in all the million little moments that happened in between. Like dancing in the kitchen and singing silly songs off-key. It was in backyard games and movie nights snuggled up under blankets. It was even in those seemingly endless drives to and from school.

As I reflect on these "small" moments, I can't help but wonder if this is what God has been waiting for me to see all along. That, yes, there are the big, grand, memory-making moments—and they can be wonderful (or terrible), inspiring (or crushing), and life-changing. But most of life is lived in the in-between. The getting up, the going, and the getting-on-with-it moments.

These are the moments when ministry really happens. The touching of lives and hearts with a truth lived out as best I can, begging for His help and apologizing when I make an utter and complete mess of an opportunity He's given me.

Yes, God is there in those larger-than-life, over-the-top, mountain-peak and depths-of-the valley moments. But the wonder and might and majesty of God—and the opportunity to share and serve Him—are just as present in all those everyday, easily missed moments. And that knowledge is shaping and changing the way I see everything. Because *every* moment is an intersection of ordinary and divine.

Oh, Father,
help me not to miss
a moment of the
ministry You've given
to me. Amen.

Reflect

Life is a ministry of moments.

It's easy to see God in the big moments of life, but do you see Him in all the in-between moments? Where and how?

_____

_____

_____

_____

_____

_____

Why is it important to see God—to seek and share Him—in all the moments of life?

_____

_____

_____

_____

_____

_____

_____

_____

Challenge

That less-than-joyful thing you need to do today?
Make it a moment of ministry.

WAITING WELL

Day 23

PROVERBS 3:5-6

Trust in the LORD with all your heart
and lean not on your own understanding;
in all your ways submit to him,
and he will make your paths straight.

WAITING IS A DAILY PART OF OUR LIVES—waiting in lines, waiting in traffic, and, of course, waiting on God and His answers.

If I'm honest, waiting is not my most favorite thing. I tend to grow impatient and pick the wrong line, the wrong lane, and the wrong answer because I don't want to wait. *(Yeah, I'm still working on that one.)* I believe God knew that about me from the start. Which is why, I suppose, when I first became a Christian in college and began memorizing Bible verses, the first one He gave me was Proverbs 3:5–6. A sort of divine preparation, if you will. It was as if God looked down from heaven at my still-bowed head and said, "She's going to need to be reminded of this one . . . *a lot.* Better get it in early."

Over the years, I've done a lot of learning. And my impatient self is slowly coming to see that there is more to waiting than minutes ticking away on a clock.

Sometimes, waiting is stillness—not the stuck-in-Nashville-traffic-and-waiting-to-move-an-inch kind of stillness. But the soul-deep stillness of a heart waiting expectantly for God's voice to speak, to comfort and sustain, and to lead.

There are other times when waiting is continuing to do what I know to be right—offering up prayers and praise to Him and giving love and kindness to others—as I wait for His answers to come.

But the one thing waiting must always, *always* be is . . . surrender. Laying down my schedule, my preferences, and my stubborn selfishness and pride. *Your will, O Lord, not mine.*

To wait well is more than waiting for God; it's waiting with Him—passionately and expectantly (Psalm 37:34). Waiting for the answers, the strength, the comfort, and the sustaining love He has promised to provide. And so I surrender, over and over again, to waiting both *for* and *with* Him at the intersection of ordinary and divine.

Lord, teach me to surrender my times of waiting to You. Amen.

Reflect

Waiting can be in stillness or in busyness,
but it must always be in surrender.

What does it mean to wait in surrender? What does that look like in your life right now?

_____

_____

_____

_____

_____

What is the difference between waiting *for* God and waiting *with* Him?
Why are both necessary?

_____

_____

_____

_____

_____

_____

_____

What are you waiting on in your life right now? In your faith? What would
it look like to wait well?

_____

_____

_____

_____

_____

_____

Challenge

That thing you're hoping for, praying for,
and waiting on—surrender it fully to Him:
Your will, O Lord, not mine.

LIKE
A
CHILD

Day 24

Truly I tell you, unless you change and become
like little children, you will never enter the
kingdom of heaven.

MY HUSBAND'S GRANDMOTHER, whom we affectionately called Granny Putt, always gave us toys for Christmas. It didn't matter how old we were. At her house, we got toys. That first year I joined the celebration and opened up my package to find a little doll tucked inside was quite a surprise!

As the guys pulled out Matchbox cars and dinosaurs, and the ladies pulled out pretend makeup kits and stuffed bears, we laughed and joked about those toys. And Granny Putt laughed along with us. We thought we were humoring her. But now, I think she was teaching us. Granny was on to something with those little toy-filled packages. They held a much bigger purpose than creating a few smiles.

Granny was remembering and recreating a little bit of that excitement and delight that is a part of childhood. And she was encouraging us to do the same. Truth is, we all looked forward to our little toys, wondering what we would get each year.

I can get so busy with the serious grown-up business of life that I can easily slip into thinking it's all up to me. The load weighs heavy and I find myself missing out on much of the wonder of a life lived with God and all the little gifts He gives.

And I think that's why Jesus told us to be like a little child in our faith. Children are naturally inquisitive, always seeking to know more and more, while also realizing they need to look to someone else for the answers. That's how I want to be. Always seeking to know more and more about this God I serve, looking to Him for the answers, and realizing that He—not I—is the One in charge.

Like a child, I can trust God to carry the weight of my burdens for me (Matthew 11:28) and to lead me to the wonders, the delights, and the joys He daily pours into my life at each intersection of ordinary and divine.

Lord, help me
to trust You with all the
grown-up business of
life and to find delight in
Your wonders . . .
just like a little child.
Amen.

How might the seriousness of being "all grown up" interfere with having a child-like faith?

_____

_____

_____

_____

If you could buy yourself a small toy today—something inexpensive—what would it be? Why not do it?

_____

_____

_____

_____

Imagine you're six years old and seeing the world around you for the first time. What fresh wonders do you see?

_____

_____

_____

_____

Challenge

Trust God with the serious stuff and let
yourself look for His wonders and delights.

WILD
VIOLETS
AND
OTHER . . .
WEEDS?

Day 25

While Jesus was having dinner at Levi's house, many tax collectors and sinners were eating with him and his disciples, for there were many who followed him.

WILD VIOLETS GROW IN A SWATH OF PURPLE and white across part of my backyard, and I adore them. So much, in fact, that I decided to transplant some of these hardy little wildflowers to one of my flowerbeds—a spot where nothing else seemed to want to grow. Not having a particularly green thumb, I searched online to see just how to do that. That's when I discovered my beloved little blooms were considered weeds! Words like *scourge, invasive,* and even *plague* peppered the articles I read. There were lengthy articles about how to get rid of them. (Most of which said, "Good luck with that!") But hardly a word was found on how to transplant and nurture them.

Oh well, "weeds" or not, I love them anyway. I dug them up and plopped them down. And I'm happy to report they're flourishing in that bed where nothing else wanted to grow. I just might add wild violets to another spot or two.

A. A. Milne, of Winnie-the-Pooh fame, has been credited with saying, "Weeds are flowers, too, once you get to know them." Though some argue the source, the words ring true, and I think Jesus would agree. After all, He has always been a collector of what many saw—and still see—as humanity's weeds. The overlooked and cast-aside, the scandalous and scorned. He not only welcomes them into His garden, but He also tends, nurtures, and heals them until they bloom. (*Forgive me, Lord, when I fail to do the same.*)

There are many reassurances for me in Jesus's gardening habits. Because I'm quite certain that once upon a time, I was a weed. (I'll even admit to still being prickly with thorns on occasion.) Yet, He has chosen me for His garden. And because I have chosen Him in return, I am as free to bloom and grow as those beautiful little wild violets . . . at the intersection of ordinary and divine.

Lord, thank You for transplanting this "weed" into the garden of Your kingdom. Amen.

Reflect

Jesus welcomes all into the garden of His kingdom, even those considered by some to be weeds.

Think of a person or situation that feels like a weed in your life. Do you think Jesus would view them the same way? How might that person or situation become a flower to you?

_____

_____

_____

_____

_____

_____

Read Romans 3:23. Do you agree that we all, at some point, have been weeds? Now, read Romans 5:8. How does it feel to know that Jesus has transplanted you into His garden? How does that change *everything*?

_____

_____

_____

_____

_____

_____

Challenge

Plant a seed today—in the earth or in someone's heart. Tend it, nurture it, and wait for it to bloom and grow.

CAPTURING
MEMORIES

Day 26

Mary treasured up all these things and pondered
them in her heart.

MY FAMILY AND I have shared some fabulous adventures. Hiking up mountain trails, riding rollercoasters (with me sometimes wishing I hadn't),
and splashing through waterfalls and waves. I have the photo albums to
prove it. (Or at least I will when I get all those pictures organized one day.)
Though I'm far from an expert, I love taking pictures to capture all these
special times. To be able to "hold" a moment in my hand and look back on
it—remembering the joy—is practically priceless to me.

Yet, when I think about the things I most love about my family and our
lives together, I usually can't point to any one of those photos. Because some
of the most treasured memories can't always be photographed. How could I,
for example, capture the simple wonder and joy of things like:

- impromptu hugs from my son
- calls just to chat from my all-grown-up-now girl
- my husband reaching out to hold my hand
- stories shared by parents and grandparents
- silly text messages between friends

No, when it comes to my life's most treasured memories, so many of
them aren't captured on film, tucked into photo albums, or saved on my
phone.

The memories of my time with God are the same way. There's no photo
of that mountain-top moment or that best-ever-day when He reached down
from heaven and whispered to me (to *me!*), "I want you to be Mine." No snapshots exist of the million-and-one different ways He has stepped into my

life—keeping His promises, revealing His presence, and listening and speaking to me (again, to *me*!). I don't have an album of His love, His mercy, or His grace. But I'm determined to make one. From this point on, I'm determined to take the pictures of those moments. If not with my camera or my phone, then with my heart.

Because I don't want to forget. I want to be able to "hold" these memories in my hand and in my heart. I want to relive the joy of them. Like Mary after the birth of Jesus, I want to scoop up and tuck away these priceless, precious snapshots of a life lived with family, with friends, and with God. So that whenever I need a reason to smile, or to be reminded of His faithfulness, I can pull out these memory books of my heart and remember how often love meets me at the intersection of ordinary and divine.

Lord, help my heart
capture all the treasures
You pour into my life.
Amen.

Reflect

Life's most treasured moments are sometimes only
captured as snapshots in our hearts.

What moments and memories with loved ones do you most treasure? Why those moments? How might you capture them in photographs—whether with the lens of a camera or the lens of your heart?

_____

_____

_____

What moments and memories of God do you most treasure? Why those moments? How might you treasure them in your heart?

_____

_____

_____

Why do you think we tend to photograph only the "big" moments when so much of life is lived in between them? Going forward, how might you change this?

_____

_____

_____

Challenge

Take out your phone and photograph the moments today. Capture the treasures of family, of friends, and of God—the moments that make you smile.

NAPS
AND
SABBATHS

Day 27

MARK 6:31

Come with me by yourselves to a quiet place
and get some rest.

SUNDAY AFTERNOONS, after church and lunch, are for naps. It's a time that my family guards rather jealously (and, at times, a bit crankily). There's something so restful about drifting off to sleep on the couch in the middle of the day with the television playing softly in the background. Yes, I know there are all those scientific studies about televisions and noise while sleeping, but for me, it sets the stage for the loveliest of afternoon naps. Curled up on the couch with my napping blanket (there's a specific one) and a snoozing puppy. It feels decidedly *decadent*. And just a little bit irresponsible.

But is it really? Decadent or irresponsible? Sunday is the Sabbath, the day of rest. Still, my desire to rest wars with all that I have to do. Whether it's tidying away the still-not-done tasks from the past week or preparing for the gotta-do-it responsibilities of the coming week. Whenever the weight of those to-dos hits me, I know I can push through the fatigue (and I sometimes do, giving in to the "need" to check just a few things off the list). But is that the best way to celebrate the Sabbath—this gift of rest God has so graciously given me?

When Jesus came, He transformed that Old Testament command to rest (Exodus 31:14) into a beautiful invitation. Because, I believe, He knew the need for rest would not go away with the changing of covenants or the passing of years. Now, He calls to us to come away with Him and find rest for our weary hearts and souls, as well as rest from our labors (Mark 6:31, Matthew 11:28).

Rest doesn't come easy for me, though. It requires a certain element of trust. Trusting that my world won't come crashing down if I step away for a bit. That everything won't implode or explode in that short time I'm not there to personally oversee it. (*How arrogant of me. Sorry, God.*)

I must remember that God is working, even as I rest (John 5:17). He is not idle. He does not sleep (Psalm 121:3–4). I can trust Him to watch over me and mine. And perhaps that's the real reason behind the command turned invitation to rest. Not so much because my body needs to rest in sleep, but because my soul needs to rest by trusting in Him.

So perhaps I should nap more often and enjoy this sleepy little intersection of ordinary and divine.

Lord, bless me with
rest and remind me that
You—and not me—
are the One Who holds
everything together.
Amen.

Reflect

God is working and holding all things together,
even when I rest.

Do you make time to rest on the Sabbath? If not, what keeps you from resting? If so, how do you rest?

_____

_____

_____

What renews and restores you? Is it a short nap, a time of stillness, or something else?

_____

_____

_____

_____

Our Sabbaths are often filled with busyness. Is yours? How might you make it more of a time of rest?

_____

_____

_____

_____

Challenge

Carve out time for rest today—whether with
a short nap, a time of sheer idleness, or whatever
renews and restores you.

STEPPING INTO HIS PRESENCE

Day 28

Let us come boldly to the throne of our gracious God.
There we will receive his mercy, and we will find grace
to help us when we need it most.

I FIND MYSELF TALKING TO GOD a lot these days. Out loud even. It's one of the benefits of working alone and from home, I suppose. (I also talk to the puppy, but his replies are a bit more predictable.) With God, I mostly share random thoughts and musings. Sometimes, it's a quick prayer for wisdom or patience, or a *Lord, what on earth do I write on this page?* kind of plea. Other times, I offer simple bits of conversation as I go along that keep me connected to Him.

But there are times when I need more. When I need the engulfing of His presence. Yes, I know I never actually *leave* His presence. He is with me always. So perhaps it's better to say that there are times when I need to be more fully *aware* of His presence. Such an awareness often takes a bit of effort on my part. I usually need stillness and silence. Which means I must shut out the noises of the world and still the riot of thoughts that seems always to be circling through my mind. No, this stepping into His presence isn't always easy, but it is getting easier with practice.

In these times with God, I pray what I suppose are the usual sorts of prayers, seeking His wisdom, guidance, mercy, and grace. I ask for reminders of who I really am in a world that loves to tell me who I am not. I lay my worries and fears at His feet . . . and I beg His forgiveness for the times when I pick them right back up again.

Mostly, though, I try to listen, sitting with Him in that stillness and silence. Awed and humbled by the fact that He invites me here, into His throne room. Doesn't He know who I am? All that I've done, and thought, and said? The beautiful truth is that He does. And yet He still chose to send

His own Son to fling wide the doors to this throne room of heaven so that I could meet with Him at this intersection of ordinary and divine made possible by the love and sacrifice of Christ.

Lord, still my thoughts. Silence the noise of the world. And help me fully step into Your presence. Amen.

Reflect

God's invitation into the throne room of His presence is not grudging; He wants and welcomes you there . . . with Him.

What does it mean to you to be able to step into God's throne room? To have a heavenly Father who will listen to and help you?

_____

_____

_____

There is no one right way to pray. How do you best connect to God in prayer?

_____

_____

_____

_____

_____

_____

Do you include listening time in your prayer life? If so, how has it made a difference? If not, how might your prayer life change if you did?

_____

_____

_____

_____

_____

_____

Challenge

Find a time to slip away, in stillness
and silence, and pray.

THE
CHAIR

Day 29

You hem me in behind and before,
and you lay your hand upon me.

I HAVE A FAVORITE CHAIR. It's an older one, but relatively new to me. A hand-me-down a couple of times over, but it "fits" me just right—with the help of a little pillow. And it rocks in a smooth and soothing rhythm. You don't so much sit in this chair as you settle into it. It is both comfortable and comforting.

I love my chair. It sits tucked into a corner of my office, with bookshelves on one side and a window to the world on the other. It is here where I meet with God each day as I read His Word, as I pray, and as I listen to His whispers that guide my way.

This love-worn chair has also become my refuge for those moments when life is just a little too much. When the whirl of everything makes my head spin and my heart beat far too fast. It's here where I'm learning to *settle*. I don't mean curling into the cushions or burrowing under a throw. Rather, I'm learning to settle *into God*. Just as falling into my chair's upholstered embrace comforts my weary limbs, the presence of God wraps around me and comforts my weary soul when I seek Him. And the peace I find is beyond anything I could ever ask for or imagine (Ephesians 3:20).

In many ways, this settling into His presence is the ultimate trust fall. It's acknowledging that while I don't have all the answers, I trust that He does. It's confessing that I can't control every little thing and believing He can. It's knowing God will not only catch me, but will also catch and take care of all that is worrying me. Because He is God, and He is good, and He is oh so good to me.

His promises and protection hem me in, before and behind. With His hand upon me, I find that I can rise up out of this chair and carry on. No longer whipped about by winds of worldly chaos but following Him as He makes a way through my storms, both big and small.

Yes, it is comfortable and comforting here in my chair, but I find even more comfort and strength when I settle into His presence at this intersection of ordinary and divine.

Lord, thank You for being the One I can settle into.

Reflect

Settling into the presence of God is settling into something far greater than could ever be asked for or imagined.

How might settling into the presence of God—and turning all the chaos of the day over to Him—be the ultimate trust fall?

_____

_____

_____

_____

How is putting aside the desire to have all the answers and be in control connected to settling into the presence of God? To embracing both His power and His presence?

_____

_____

_____

_____

_____

_____

_____

God is God, He is good, and He is in control. How could these truths help you navigate even the busiest, craziest day?

_____

_____

_____

_____

_____

_____

Challenge

Create a space in your home where you can settle—
mind, body, and soul—into the presence of God.

WHEN IT DOESN'T FEEL LIKE HOLY GROUND

Day 30

We know that in all things God works for the
good of those who love him, who have been called
according to his purpose.

I HAVE COME TO BELIEVE that every step we take lands us on holy ground. Because, as a child of God, His Spirit lives within me and, thus, travels with me everywhere I go. But I'll admit there are those times when the place where I'm standing doesn't feel all that holy.

Those moments hit when the disappointments are huge and heavy, when the diagnosis isn't what I'd hoped, and when the loss is keen. They swirl in with the whirlwinds of little disasters—the lost keys, the sick dog, and the ringing phone when I'm already running so, so late. They stalk in when the peace is disturbed by that someone who just loves disturbing the peace. And they creep in with the doubts and uncertainties that whisper, *Who do you think you are?*

When the ground is muddy with tears or frozen with frustrations, when the storm clouds roll in, when God is hard to see . . . these are the times when the place where I'm standing doesn't feel like holy ground.

And yet it is.

It would be so easy to falter in these moments—and don't we all sometimes? But I know in my heart that this is the time to fight even harder for my faith and to ask God to fight for me. The answer isn't in faltering; it's in falling to my knees as I lift up my face to the heavens and plead, *Lord, I know You are here. Even in this. Show me, Lord, just a glimpse to get me through.*

And He does.

Sometimes His answer is big and bold and shining like the noonday sun. Other times it's subtle, waiting to be searched out and found. He might work to fix the situation, changing it to be what He knows I need it to be.

Or—more often, it seems—He will fix me, changing *me* to be what He knows I need to be.

Whatever the answer, whatever the need, whatever way He chooses to work, I can carry on because He stands with me. And I will praise Him here on this spot of holy ground at the intersection of ordinary and divine.

Lord, remind me that You are here . . . even here.

Reflect

God always fixes. Sometimes He fixes the situation, but more often He fixes us.

Whether it's the huge and heavy or the little whirlwinds of daily disasters, what are the moments or situations that feel less than holy in your life? How do you find your way through those times?

_____

_____

_____

_____

_____

Instead of God using you to change a situation, have you ever experienced
God using a situation to change you? Record that story here.

_____

_____

_____

_____

_____

_____

Consider the words of Romans 8:28. How have you seen this truth play out
in your own life?

_____

_____

_____

_____

_____

Challenge

When the ground where you're standing
doesn't feel so holy, seek the One who has the
power to make all things holy.

MORNING WALKS AND ENDLESS DISCOVERIES

Day 31

O Lord, what a variety of things you have made!
In wisdom you have made them all.
The earth is full of your creatures.

MORNING WALKS WERE ONCE FOR EXERCISE. A brisk pace. A few laps. Increased heart rate. Up the inclines and down the hills.

Then, along came a puppy. *Beanie.*

Now morning walks are no longer for exercise. At least not mine. The pace is slower. The laps fewer. The heart rate calmer. And those hills? Well, sometimes his short little legs can't quite make the climb, and he needs to be carried the rest of the way home.

Most days, my walks no longer even feel like exercise. Still—though the exercise experts would probably disagree—I think allowing pupster to set the pace has been good for me. For one thing, morning walks are no longer just another item to check off my list.

Walks are now a lesson in patience, as Mr. Curiosity stops to smell every single mailbox, *almost* every roadside tree, and dozens of random clumps of grass. He will not be hurried. Our walks are a surrender to the slower pace of discovery. Every leaf skittering across his path, every bird fluttering through the trees, and every squirrel chattering as it taunts just out of reach must be investigated. Each step is an adventure into delight and somewhere new to explore.

All of which gives me plenty of time for my own exploring. I discover things I've probably passed a hundred times before but never noticed. Like the wild lamb's ear growing near the edge of a ravine (and now happily growing in my front flowerbed). Or the way the sun slices through the shadows of the trees. I've found hawk's feathers and new-to-me varieties of wildflowers.

And those leaves that skitter across our path? They're now an endless source of delight to me, too.

As I slow my pace, I witness the endless creativity of God all around me. And no doubt because of the slower pace, I better hear His whispers to me.

No, morning walks might not provide as much exercise for my body as they once did. But they exercise my soul as Beanie and I explore together all these lovely intersections of ordinary and divine.

Lord, thank You for puppies and wildflowers and skittering leaves— and for all the endless wonders that remind me of You! Amen.

Reflect

A slower pace allows time for exploring the wonders of God and space for hearing His whispers.

Have you ever been forced into a slower pace? What frustrations does that cause? What blessings does it bring?

_____

_____

_____

_____

_____

_____

Are there things like morning walks or even times of prayer that have become just another thing to check off the list? How can you reclaim those times for God today?

_____

_____

_____

_____

_____

Challenge

Take a walk and let it become an adventure
of exploration and discovery, of seeking
out the wonders of God.

WHEN I
FORGET

Day 32

I, the LORD, made you, and I will not forget you.

I FORGET. *SO MANY THINGS*. And in one of those horribly ironic twists, it seems the more I need to remember, the more I forget. Names. Passwords and pin numbers. Where I've put my glasses. In one particularly memorable moment of forgetting, I ranted to my daughter about not being able to find my phone. And yes, as you've probably guessed, I was talking to her on it.

Since I recognize my weakness of forgetfulness, I try to set myself up for success by scribbling notes on post-its, calendar pages, and napkins—whatever's handy. I set up reminders and dictate into apps. I create silly mnemonic devices for remembering names: Kay is okay, and Dorothy is off to see the wizard. (Word to the wise: don't start mumbling those mnemonic devices until you are well out of hearing range of the person whose name you are trying to remember. Otherwise, it can get awkward. Don't ask how I know.) I try all of these little tricks, but then I *forget* to look at the notes or listen to the app, and the mnemonics get all mixed up. *Sigh.*

My theory is that there are just too many things to remember.

The thing I most often seem to forget, though, is that God has got this—whatever the "this" might be at the moment. Whether it's helping me through the awkward *What* is *that person's name?* moment or something much more monumental, God is ultimately in control. I can trust Him with my path, my past, my future, my present forgetfulness, and all my problems. Because He is the One who can actually see it all, handle it all, fix it all, and guide me through it all—even the things I've forgotten to remember. Nothing is too difficult for Him (Matthew 19:26).

God always remembers me. And with so much patience, mercy, and grace, He uses even my forgetful moments to remind me of how much I need Him and to draw me closer to Him with these intersections of ordinary and divine.

Forgive me, God, when I forget to remember You. Amen.

Reflect

God not only always remembers us, but He also uses our struggles to remind us that He is here.

Do you sometimes struggle to remember that it is really God who is in control? Is it difficult to entrust life's chores and challenges to His care? Why?

_____

_____

_____

_____

_____

_____

_____

What helps you remember God in the day-to-day moments of life?

_____

_____

_____

_____

_____

_____

Challenge

Write a memo, dictate a note, or set a reminder to remember to spend time with God each day this week.

MIDNIGHT MOMENTS

Day 33

Be still, and know that I am God.

FOR SO LONG, nights were interrupted by the needs of little ones—and by my own need to reassure myself that they were sleeping safely.

That need for reassurance often sent me creeping down the hall to take a peek at my babies. But no matter how silently I stepped, they almost always sensed my approach. A little head would pop up—and *I'd* hit the floor with ninja-like reflexes, belly-crawling out of the room with a stealth any special forces soldier would be proud to claim. I knew if I were spotted, an escape from the crib would become not just an option for my little one, but a necessity.

There were times, though, when my presence in those middle-of-the-night hours *was* a necessity. And while part of me longed for a return to my own bed and to sleep, another part of me treasured those midnight moments. When all was still and quiet and the house was wrapped in a blanket of soft shadows.

A sort of sacredness filled those dark, silent hours as I held my sleepy little one. Though half asleep myself, I cherished the bundle of warmth in my arms, breathing in the lingering scents of bath time. Often, I rocked far longer than needed so that I could savor those holy moments just a little longer.

Now that my children are grown, those midnight moments still happen—prompted now by the restlessness of growing older and sometimes nudged awake by the Spirit to pray. Rather than becoming frustrated, I'm learning to embrace these moments once again. To settle back into My Father's arms, and to rest and listen to Him. When all is still and quiet. When I can be still and quiet.

Psalm 46:10 says, "Be still, and know that [He] is God." But there is more to stillness than simply not moving. Other translations deepen the meaning with phrases like "cease striving" (NASB) and "let be and be still" (AMPC).

Be still, cease striving, let be. All calls to lay down my troubles, my worries, and my strivings. To let God be God. Here in these midnight moments of intersection between ordinary and divine.

Lord, teach me to be still, to cease striving, and to let You be God of all my moments. Amen.

Reflect

Midnight moments offer a sort of sacred stillness that can often be elusive in the light of day.

What wakes you up in the night? What thoughts thread through your mind in those moments?

_____

_____

_____

Consider the words of Psalm 46:10 in the different translations: *be still, cease striving,* and *let be.* Which translation most resonates with you? Why?

_____

_____

_____

_____

_____

What does it mean to know that God is God? Does that knowledge impact your awake-in-the-night moments? How is it linked to being still?

_____

_____

_____

_____

_____

_____

=== Challenge ===

When you find yourself awake in those
midnight moments, take that time to be still
and know that He is God.

REVERIE
IN THE
REPETITION

Day 34

Praise be to the God and Father of our
Lord Jesus Christ, the Father of compassion
and the God of all comfort.

SO MUCH OF MY LIFE SEEMS to play on repeat. A never-ending circle of routines and repetition. Do you ever feel the same? Wash, tidy, fix, repeat. Work, eat, sleep, repeat. Wash, dry, repeat. This was even more true in the years when the kids were little.

Repeat. Repeat. Repeat.

For far too long, the sameness of the routines bothered me. Especially when it was accompanied by a lack of notice or appreciation. That's less true now. In part because I'm discovering a certain kind of stability and even comfort in those repetitive tasks. So much is changing in this world and in my life—and so rapidly—that a bit of predictability is welcome. In fact, the more chaotic my day, the more I turn to my routines.

And the more I notice God meeting me there.

Perhaps that's why the disciples went fishing on that long-ago night when their world was turned upside down. When their Savior was crucified, when rumors of His missing body swirled around, when the impossibility of His resurrection proved possible, when He miraculously appeared in that locked room (John 20–21). The disciples' world was in chaos. So they returned to the boats and the lake and the comfort of the routine they knew. Throw out the nets, haul them in, repeat. Throw out, haul in, repeat.

Repeat, repeat, repeat.

And Jesus met them there.

The "fix" wasn't in the fishing. And it wasn't in the routine—after all, they didn't catch a thing on their own. Rather, I think it's in the fact that they stopped trying to figure everything out on their own. And *that* made room for Jesus to step in.

In the same way, the "fix" for my crazy days isn't in the cleaning, filing, or putting away. But the repetition slows the swirl of thoughts through my head. It makes room for Jesus. It offers freedom to ponder, pray, and praise. To consider the wonders of a God who is greater than anything I could ever imagine—and who is blessing me with more than I could ever ask or imagine.

So, I'm finding a sort of peaceful reverie in these repetitions of life's routines. And I'm finding yet another intersection of ordinary and divine.

Lord, when I'm weary of the routines and repetition, help me to see the opportunity for reverie in them. Amen.

Reflect

Repetition and routines make room for God.

What are the routines, or the repetitive tasks and chores, that make up your day? Where do your thoughts go during these times? How could you use those routine, repetitive times to make room for God?

_____

_____

_____

_____

_____

_____

Do you ever find yourself turning to the routine and repetition for comfort? Do you sense God stepping into those times? How could you deepen the connection?

_____

_____

_____

_____

_____

_____

Challenge

Allow the routines of today to make
intentional room for God.

TASTE
AND
SEE

Day 35

Taste and see that the Lṭṇḋ is good.
Oh, the joys of those who take refuge in him!

I LIVE WITH A BUNCH OF PICKY EATERS. *No onions or peppers, please. No pasta for this one. No casseroles for that one.* And their tastes change! No one warns you about that little delight. What was once the best food that dear loved ones of mine ever put in their mouth suddenly morphs into the most disgusting thing on the planet. This unfortunate phenomenon usually happens without warning, and right after I've stocked up on a two-week supply. (I, myself, eat all the things I cook without complaining. Of course, I only cook the things I like. That's one of the perks of being the cook. But I'd *really* prefer the foods not touch each other on my plate, thank you.)

All this pickiness can make cooking tough. Over the years, I've learned to improvise, adding a little of this, leaving out that, and substituting as needed. It feels a bit like winning the World Cup when everyone agrees that dinner is good. Because I do find satisfaction in nourishing others, especially the ones gathered around my table. And there's joy in seeing them savor the dishes I've set before them.

I wonder if that is how God feels when I taste and savor His goodness. When I praise Him for all He's poured into my life—unmerited grace, unimaginable mercy, unending love. Even if God did nothing but save me—picky and imperfect wretch that I am—from the evil one for eternity, His goodness would still be immeasurable. And I would have reason to praise Him all the days of my life.

Yet God chooses to do so much more than "just" save me. He fills my life with people I love and who love me in return. He gifts me with a home and food and clothes. He surrounds me with the beauty and wonder of His creation. He works in all the details of my days—*personally*—helping me to be all He created me to be. He guides, encourages, strengthens, heals, comforts, and holds. The whole earth—my whole life—is filled with the goodness of God (Psalm 33:5).

And the taste of God and His gifts is so very sweet . . . at all the different intersections of ordinary and divine.

Lord, help my life to be a living praise of Your goodness. Amen.

Reflect

There is nothing so sweet as the goodness of God.

God's goodness could have stopped with salvation, but it didn't. Why do you believe He continually pours His goodness into and over us? What verses support your belief?

_____

_____

_____

_____

_____

Where do you "taste and see" the goodness of God?

_____

_____

_____

_____

_____

_____

_____

Read Psalm 145:4–7. What stories will you tell of the goodness of God?
Record one here.

_____

_____

_____

_____

_____

_____

Challenge

As you savor the flavors of your food today, consider
the sweet goodness of God and His gifts.

CALENDARS, LOAVES, AND FISH

Day 36

Jesus then took the loaves, gave thanks, and
distributed to those who were seated as much as they
wanted. He did the same with the fish.

AS MUCH AS I MIGHT LIKE to fill my days with wandering along park paths or curling up with a book, my calendar tells me there is work to be done. Too often, there is too much work to be done. Demands and deadlines are written in red, circled, highlighted, and underlined. They press in and stress out, especially when I've said "yes" far too often and "no" not nearly enough.

It's okay. I've got a plan, I reassure myself. But inevitably, something shifts—an emergency, a delay, a need-it-now demand—and my carefully laid plans for getting it all done crumble like a house of cards caught in the winds of a Tennessee tornado. Even my must-not-miss-this quiet times with God get rushed through, or, I'll confess, even occasionally skipped. (Tell me I'm not alone in this struggle.)

Interestingly enough, when I look at the life and ministry of Jesus, I see that He was often busy. Even to the point of not having time to eat (Mark 6:30–31). How did Jesus handle the busyness of this business of life? The key, I think, is that although He was busy, Jesus was busy with the things of God—the things that served Him and brought others to Him.

That, then, is my challenge: to be busy with the things of God. To lay out the tasks and commitments for His inspection *before* I add them to my to-do list. When I pause long enough to do this, the difference is astonishing. Am I still busy? Yes! Am I still tired at the end of the day? Absolutely. But it's the peaceful tired that comes from a day spent with God, doing the things that serve Him and bring others to Him.

When I pause long enough to follow this practice, my calendar, rather than being clouded with red, offers room to breathe. And my time, rather than being stretched too thin, becomes like the little boy's loaves and fish: offered up to God and made more than enough at the intersection of ordinary and divine.

Lord, help me remember that my time is really Yours. I offer it up to You now. Guide me to what matters most to You. Amen.

Reflect

Jesus was busy with the things of God—the things that served Him and brought others to Him.

It's easy to put off God because He doesn't demand or yell or send urgent emails. So how do you hold yourself accountable to daily time with Him?

_____

_____

_____

_____

_____

_____

_____

Often, much of the daily business of life doesn't feel like ministry. How can you transform those tasks of job and home and family into time spent with and for God?

_____

_____

_____

_____

_____

_____

Challenge

Lay out in prayer the tasks and commitments
of the day for God's inspection *before* adding
them to your to-do list.

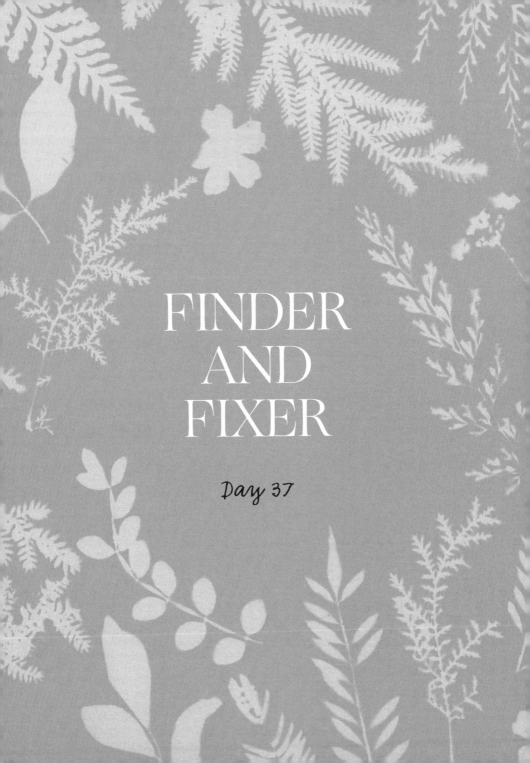

FINDER
AND
FIXER

Day 37

She did what she could. She poured perfume on my
body beforehand to prepare for my burial.

I TEND TO BE THE FINDER and fixer in the family. If it's lost or someone just can't find whatever they're looking for, they ask me. If it's broken, they bring it to me. And, honestly, there's not a lot of stuff I haven't been able to fix with a little glue, some duct tape, and maybe a YouTube video or two.

But when my son was little, he brought me something I couldn't fix. A little piece of his toy truck had broken off. It was hard plastic and tiny, and no amount of glue was going to stick those pieces back together again with any kind of lasting power. I tried anyway. I applied a little glue and added a little tape. It wasn't going to fix the brokenness for long, but I did what I could do.

Sometimes, I have to accept that's all I can do. Because there are times in life when I can fix and find and make everything as good as new. But then there are times when I can't. In *those* times, my task is to do what I can do, even if it doesn't fix the brokenness with any kind of lasting power.

Much like the woman in Mark 14. Her actions are a picture of humility, of gratitude beyond words, and of someone who did what she could do. She knew Jesus was in danger. She knew the Pharisees were looking for any reason to arrest Him. She knew they wanted to silence forever the One who had saved her. And she knew her actions wouldn't fix the world's brokenness with any kind of lasting power. But . . . she could kneel before her Savior. She could anoint His head with costly perfume. She could take these precious moments in His presence and worship Him.

So she did what she could do. And Jesus said that was enough.

I think about her often, especially when facing one of those things I can't fix or find. Little toy trucks, fractured relationships, problems far too big for me to solve. In those moments, I remember that, like her, I can still

156

do what I can do. And I can trust Jesus to make it enough, as He always does at the intersection of ordinary and divine.

Lord, please give me
the courage to do what
I can do and to trust the
outcome to You. Amen.

Reflect

Sometimes we can only do what we can do
and trust Jesus to make it enough.

When you know a problem can't be "fixed" with any kind of lasting power, are you tempted to turn away and ignore it? Why is it important to do what you can do, even if it doesn't completely fix everything?

_____

_____

_____

_____

_____

Might there be times when "doing what you can do" means *not* swooping in to fix everything, but rather allowing someone to wrestle through? What could you still do in such situations?

_____

_____

_____

_____

_____

Is there an "unfixable" in your life? A problem, situation, or relationship? What is something that you can still do? How can you entrust the outcome to God?

_____

_____

_____

_____

_____

_____

_____

Challenge

When you're asked to fix or to find, remember that long-ago woman and just do what you can do.

THE
FRAGRANCE
OF FAITH

Day 38

Our lives are a Christ-like fragrance rising up to God.

SCIENCE TELLS US that our sense of smell is intricately interwoven with our thoughts and memories. I know from experience that this is true.

For example, the smell of cornbread hot from the oven pops me right back into my granny's kitchen, while the sweet scent of honey is an instant trip to the backyard where my grandfather kept his hives of bees. God fills His creation with fragrances, and those fragrances so easily become scent-filled reminders of the moments of our lives. Like the rich, wet smell of a waterfall that calls me to that moment when His heart spoke to mine. Baby lotion, pencil shavings, Play-Doh, and certain colognes also have their own specific memories attached. Some are wonderful and comforting and wholly welcome, while others bring less pleasant memories to mind.

We, too, fill the world around us with a fragrance. One that has nothing to do with perfumes or colognes, and everything to do with the way we live our lives—especially in those moments of stress, frustration, and fear. Which makes me wonder . . . what "fragrance" am I leaving behind? Is it the stench of sharp words and a short temper? Is it the cold, icy scent of indifference? Or is it the sweet smell of God's kindness, patience, and love?

In every situation, I want the impressions I make with my words and my actions—and the memories they create in others—to be fragrant with faith and the love of Christ. Such a life can be risky, I know. For while that sweet fragrance will call to those who are knowingly (or unknowingly) seeking Him and His peace for themselves, that same fragrance is certain to repel others—or even encourage attack. Perhaps because it reminds them of the God they aren't yet ready to serve.

Nevertheless, I believe the Word when it tells me that to God, a life of faith and obedience and love is the fragrance of worship and praise. A scent-filled reminder of His Son and all that binds me to Him at the intersection of ordinary and divine.

Lord, please wash away the stench of my own selfishness and soak me in the sweet fragrance of Your love. Amen.

Reflect

The sweet fragrance of a life lived for God is its own kind of worship and praise.

What scents bring sweet memories to mind? What scents do you avoid because of the memories associated with them? What fragrances remind you of God?

_____

_____

_____

_____

_____

What "fragrances" do you leave behind in good moments and in bad? Are they fragrances that would be pleasing to God? Are there changes you'd like to make?

_____

_____

_____

_____

_____

Challenge

When moments of stress, frustration,
or fear come your way, pause and consider the
fragrance you want to leave behind. Let it be
the fragrance of the love of God.

COUNTING
CONTENTMENTS

Day 39

This is the day the LORD has made.
We will rejoice and be glad in it.

IT'S A GRAY, MISTY SORT OF DAY as I sit here looking out my kitchen window. The sweet, spicy smell of apple cake wraps around me and chases the chills away. There's a family potluck this afternoon, and I've been assigned a dessert.

The puppy sleeps on a chair beside me, occasionally lifting his head to half-heartedly *woof* at whatever unheard-by-me sound has captured his attention. But only Ernie the mailman and his supply of treats could induce Beanie into actually leaving his cozy spot.

There are a few chores to tackle before I leave for the party. Floors to be swept, rugs to be washed, and the dishwasher is waiting—as always—to be emptied and filled again.

Instead of checking these things off my list, I choose to sit and contemplate the complete sense of contentment that envelopes me. I suppose I'm counting my blessings—or rather, I'm counting my contentments—on an ordinary day that perhaps isn't so ordinary after all.

My life is rich with so many ordinary, extraordinary blessings. Family, home, food. Laughter and gathering with those I love. Sleeping puppies and comfy kitchen chairs. Apple cakes and—most of all—a God who loves to dip into the details of my day. How can I not lift up my eyes to the hills outside my kitchen window and praise Him?

Sure, there are troubles, some worries, and even a few fears rattling around at the back of my mind. But I'm banishing them there for now, leaving them with God. I know they'll sneak out later—or I'll snatch them back myself—and then I'll have to purposefully banish them back again. It's what I do, and it's what I'm trying so hard to learn *not* to do anymore.

As I finish scribbling these words down, capturing them on a scrap of an old receipt before they disappear into the gray mist, the chores still need to be done and the timer on the oven is about to beep. But for a few moments, I'm sitting and savoring and rejoicing in this extraordinary, ordinary Saturday that the Lord made for me at the intersection of ordinary and divine.

Thank You, Lord, for blessings that are just too many to name. Amen.

How might noticing the extraordinary blessings in even the most ordinary of days help you cultivate a contented heart?

_____

_____

_____

_____

_____

Pour out your praises to God here for the blessings—the contentments—in your life. Don't overthink. Just let them spill from the overflow of your heart.

_____

_____

_____

_____

_____

_____

Read Psalm 103. How many gifts do you find in this one psalm? How could these gifts help you, like Paul, to be content "in any and every situation" (Philippians 4:12)?

_____

_____

_____

_____

_____

_____

=== Challenge ===

Pause here and now. Look around. See. Notice.
Breathe in. Name just a few of the contentments
of God that surround you.

THEREFORE

Day 40

Therefore everyone who hears these words of mine
and puts them into practice is like a wise man who
built his house on the rock.

I'VE TAUGHT BIBLE CLASSES for years now. Some for children, some for adults. No matter the age group, I love sharing the joy, hope, and peace I find in God's Word. And while I make sure every lesson explores the truths and true stories of the Bible, there's one other thing I believe is essential to include: the *therefores*.

Therefore is a conjunction, a joining or connecting word. It joins God's truths with the changes I need to make and the actions I need to take. Because "head knowledge" of the Bible's concepts and commands isn't enough. Even the evil one knows these things (Matthew 4:6). What matters is how I allow that knowledge to change me. And it's the *therefores* that compel me to make those changes.

Sometimes it's a call to change who I believe I am: *"Therefore,* if anyone is in Christ, the new creation has come: The old has gone, the new is here!" (2 Corinthians 5:17).

Other times, it's a call to soften my heart and change my attitude: *"Therefore,* as God's chosen people, holy and dearly loved, clothe yourselves with compassion, kindness, humility, gentleness and patience" (Colossians 3:12).

It can be a command that compels me to take action: *"Therefore* go and make disciples of all nations, baptizing them in the name of the Father and of the Son and of the Holy Spirit" (Matthew 28:19).

And then there are those beautiful passages in which *therefore* is both a promise to claim and a foundation to build a life and a faith upon: *"Therefore,* there is now no condemnation for those who are in Christ Jesus" (Romans 8:1).

Perhaps you began reading these devotions with the hope of boosting your faith or gaining a fresh perspective on His timeless truths. Perhaps God has felt far away and you longed to draw near to Him. Or perhaps God has felt nearer than before, and you wanted a resource to help you deepen that connection.

Whatever your motivation and wherever your relationship with God is right now, as you close the pages of this little book, I pray that He will shine a light onto some new truth—big or small—and that it will become a "therefore" in your own life. A therefore that sends you seeking Him in His Word and in every moment . . . and finding Him always at the intersection of ordinary and divine.

Lord, help my life to be an answer to all Your "therefores." Amen.

Reflect

Therefore is a call to allow the truths of God's Word to change our hearts and lives.

Why is "head knowledge" of God and His Word not enough? Why do we need the *therefores*?

_____

_____

_____

_____

_____

_____

Choose one of the verses from today's reading and fill in the following blanks. Be sure to make your responses both personal and specific.

Because God _____

_____

therefore, I will _____

_____

_____ .

─══ *Challenge* ══─

Search the Bible for God's *therefores*
and take note of what you find.

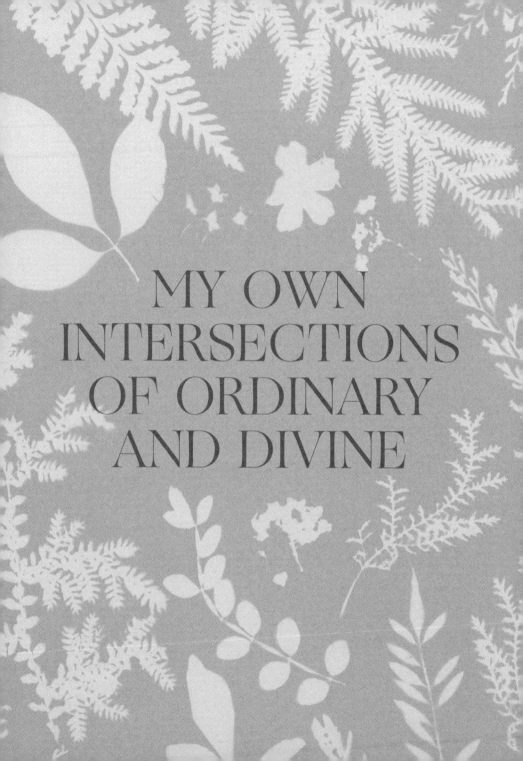

MY OWN
INTERSECTIONS
OF ORDINARY
AND DIVINE

PRAYERS OFFERED

1 JOHN 5:14

This is the confidence we have in approaching God:
that if we ask anything according to his will,
he hears us.

PRAYERS ANSWERED

ISAIAH 65:24

Before they call I will answer;
while they are still speaking I will hear.

_____

_____

_____

_____

_____

_____

_____

_____

_____

_____

_____

_____

_____

_____

_____

_____

MY OWN
EVERYDAY JOYS

INTERSECTIONS OF ORDINARY AND DIVINE I WANT TO REMEMBER